Dr. Matthew Harris Talks about the Temple & Priesthood Ban

Introduction

Welcome to Gospel Tangents. I'm your host Rick Bennett. Please consider donating or purchasing a transcript by going to our website https://GospelTangents.com/shop . You'll help support other documentaries and podcasts such as this.

I'd like to introduce Dr. Matt Harris. He has done a lot of Mormon history work and he's not very well-known, but I think he will be, especially after he finishes his upcoming books. We will talk about some of these books that he has published, as well as his future books. We're also going to talk about the history of the ban. With the 40th anniversary of the removal of the ban coming up here in just a few weeks, this will be a very timely interview. Dr. Matt Harris has some really interesting insights and it is going to reveal some really cool, historical information.

We will talk about President McKay's first thoughts to end the ban in 1955, Elder Hugh B. Brown's attempts to end the ban in the 1960s (and almost succeeding in 1969), some behind the curtain conversations with President Kimball, and how he persuaded the apostles to lift the ban. We will also talk about who wrote Official Declaration 2, ending the ban. It's one of my favorite interviews yet. Check out our conversation….

Contents

Before 1978: LDS Policies for Bi-racial Families in Brazil & South Africa

GT: Welcome to *Gospel Tangents Podcast*. I'm really excited to meet with Dr. Matt Harris here at Colorado State University-Pueblo. This is my farthest interview yet. I've talked to somebody from Australia,[1] and somebody from Italy,[2][3] but this is my farthest away yet. We're here in Pueblo, Colorado. So, Matt, could you introduce yourself to our audience?

Matt: Yes, Matt Harris is my name. I have been teaching here since 2005. I started my professional career at Dixie State University in southern Utah. I went to BYU for a bachelors and a master's degree in history, and another master's degree and Ph.D. at Syracuse University in Syracuse, New York.

GT: Go Orange!

Matt chuckles: Yes!

GT: Well cool! I have to say I think you, and I'm going to try to flatter you a little bit here, but I really believe this. I think you are one of the gems in the Mormon history community that people don't know yet, {Matt chuckles} and I feel like I have discovered you!

Matt chuckles: Uh oh.

GT: Because I feel like you are doing some awesome work in Mormon history.

---

[1] See our interview with Simon Southerton:
https://gospeltangents.com/2018/05/02/simon-southerton-talks-dna-excommunication/

[2] See our interview with Ugo Perego:
https://gospeltangents.com/2017/08/23/dna-101-dr-ugo-perego/

[3] Both Simon Southerton of Australia and Ugo Perego of Italy were visiting Utah when I visited with them.

Matt: Thanks.

GT: So, could you talk a little bit about some of the projects you are working on?

Matt: Yes, in 2015 I published a book with Newell Bringhurst,[4] called the *Mormon Church and Blacks: A Documentary History*.[5] That was my first foray into Mormon studies. I started my career as early American scholar. I did a book on the founding fathers and religion in American history[6], and then also a book with a BYU professor named Jay Buckley on Thomas Jefferson and Zebulon Pike and the exploration of the American West.[7]

Then I caught the Mormon history bug and did the black and Mormon book in 2015, and I've been working on several projects since then. I have two books on Ezra Taft Benson that will be published next year. I have a book on a collection of essays that I have edited with Newell Bringhurst on the Gospel Topics essays, which is very fascinating. Finally, my big project that I am really excited about is a second book on the LDS Church and Blacks since World War II. I have three chapters written, and that will be out, who knows when that will be out? {chuckles} 2019 maybe.

GT: Ok, well that's interesting because that's actually the topic I really want to talk to you about today. But two books on Ezra Taft Benson? Is this going to be like a Quinn tome?

---

[4] See our interview with Newell Bringhurst at https://wp.me/p8l6gx-oQ
[5] Can be purchased at https://amzn.to/2IAPgq4
[6] The book is called *The Founding Fathers and the Debate over Religion in Revolutionary America: A History in Documents* and is found at https://amzn.to/2Iz4SdC
[7] The book is called *Zebulon Pike, Thomas Jefferson, and the Opening of the American West* and is found at https://amzn.to/2rDoiDI

Matt chuckles: No, no, no.

GT: It doesn't fit in one book, so you've got to do two?

Matt: Well, the first book is a documentary history of Elder Benson, and it is a lengthy introduction, probably a 100-page introduction, which is strange for an introduction.

GT: Wow, that is long.

Matt: It's a contextual essay. The book is a collection of documents that have never been published on Benson's life. His FBI files, part of those are published. Letters to the John Birch Society president, he was very good friends with Robert Welch, Bob Welch is his name. Also, oral histories that were down with the family; a lot of stuff from the Eisenhower collection library, which is where the Benson family deposited the agricultural papers with Ezra Taft Benson in the early 2000s. A lot of documents that have never been published before, that's the first book.

The second book, I have edited a collection of essays on Elder Benson. It's about his rise in politics in the Eisenhower administration; also, as a significant conservative leader after World War II. Most people don't realize that he was a presidential candidate, and that he was very, very close with Barry Goldwater, one of the conservative intellectuals, or leaders I should say, politicians after World War II. Then of course, Benson as a churchman. We can, I'm sure talk about in a minute, Benson didn't make a whole lot of distinction between his politics and his religion.

So, it's a collection of essays from folks at BYU in Provo, BYU in Idaho, I did an essay. Let's see, who else? Goodness, Matthew Bowman did an essay. He is a very good scholar; Newell Bringhurst, Gary Bergera, a wide range of people contributed to this volume, and so I'm excited about it.

GT: Yeah, it sounds cool.

Matt: It will be published next year.

GT: What I would like to talk to you about today, although I think we are going to have to schedule more than one interview. You have got a lot of interesting stuff. So, I think we will cover a little bit of Benson, because that relates to kind of what I would really like to talk about is black Mormon history from World War II to the present. Obviously, that overlaps with President Benson, or Elder Benson, Apostle Benson, quite a bit. So, I'm sure we will get into that a little bit today. As far as I know, to me when I think of World War II, 1941-45, I know when we think about black history, 1949 was a big, important statement. Is that kind of where your book is going to start?

Matt: A little bit before that. After World War II, or even during World War II, President McKay, I guess he was First Counselor then, but anyway the First Presidency starts to think about expanding the church globally.[8] After the war, it really kicks into high gear. They recognize, or course, that if you're going to expand the church globally, it presents some challenges if the priesthood ban doesn't allow African nations to control their own destiny, govern their own churches.

The Church is already in South Africa by this point. This is really the first time where President McKay, who is now the church president, experiences the difficulty of bringing the gospel to a nation where there is a strong biracial

---

[8] For an interesting recap of the LDS Church in Germany, see our interview with Dr. David Nelson. He discusses Pres. McKay and J. Reuben Clark's role in Germany during World War II: https://gospeltangents.com/2017/12/17/j-reuben-clarks-harsh-feelings-about-jews/

component, and it becomes very challenging when the mission president and the missionaries are trying to determine who has, as they put it in those days, "negro blood." Anyway, they write letters to President McKay and it forces him and his counselors and the governing leadership in the church, what do we do about this problem as the missionaries and mission president try to determine who ought to hold the priesthood and who shouldn't.

So, that's the first thing. Brazil is also a challenge after the war. They have been in Brazil for quite some time after World War II, and Brazil has this heavy bi-racial component, even more so than in South Africa. Between those two countries, it forces church leadership into some very interesting predicaments. President McKay gives it a lot of thought and decides to keep the ban in the 1950s. But there were some intense discussions even then about lifting the ban.

GT: Oh wow, that early?

Matt: Yes, that early.

GT: Because I know in Greg Prince's book,[9] he talks a little bit about a situation in South Africa with the mission president. Are you familiar with that?

Matt: Yes.

GT: Could you tell us a little be more about that and how that relates to the ban?

Matt: Yes, so President Evan P. Wright is his name. He writes President McKay and he said we have got this problem. What do we do?

---

[9] Can be purchased at https://amzn.to/2wyuUsX

President McKay will travel to South Africa to visit with the mission. When he is in South Africa meeting with President Wright and the missionaries, he will see things up close and personal as it were, and the challenges of bringing the gospel to these folks who may have black blood in them, as they said. So, he decides to reverse the policy that had been in place for years. It really catches some of the leaders in Salt Lake off guard, because President McKay does it unilaterally. The policy is that people in South Africa, they no longer have to trace their genealogy out of Africa in order to prove that they have Caucasian bloodlines.

What that means is that before that happens, if you were a convert, a prospective convert to the church and you got baptized, which is ok. It didn't matter if you were African-American—or African with negro blood....

GT interrupts: They were not American, African.

Matt: Yes, it wouldn't be African-American, would it. So, African blood we'll say, if you fell under the parameters of the priesthood restriction, you could still get baptized. You just couldn't get ordained into the Melchizedek Priesthood, Aaronic or Melchizedek.

So, what President McKay does, you no longer have to trace your genealogy out of Africa, because it created a tremendous burden on the South African mission. They had diverted a number of their missionaries for proselytizing to doing genealogy work, trying to determine who had negroid blood. That was just a tremendous burden on the missionaries of the South African mission. So, when President McKay reversed that policy, he sent a letter back to the Twelve. This is what I have done. Usually this is a deliberative body, so President McKay was wont to do stuff like this occasionally. He would make these unilateral policy changes, but nonetheless, he makes this change.

What it means is that if there is no compelling evidence that you have black blood, negroid blood, then we will ordain you to the priesthood. So, for example if it is clear that your grandfather is from Africa then you have black blood then you can't be ordained. The restriction applies to you. But if you don't know, then we are going to err on the side of "We don't think the ban applies to you." We will give you the priesthood.

So, it's a fundamental change in policy that President McKay implements. President Wright, or course, is happy with it because it allows his missionaries to get back on the streets again and not have to spend most of their time trying to figure out genealogy lines, and where these folks come from.

GT: Now how long was that policy in place before President McKay got rid of it?

Matt: Good question, probably since the 1930s, early '40s maybe.

GT: So, 10-20 years maybe, in that range.

Matt: Probably so, yes. Because the church had been very reluctant to move into these nations, because of the priesthood ban. Even as early as 1938, J. Reuben Clark who was in the First Presidency, a very powerful, influential counselor, President Clark will say, "I know we are [ordaining] people in Brazil that have negroid blood. I know we are doing it." Of course, he didn't like it, but he recognized how difficult it was to determine ancestry.

Brazil was something a little bit different. There was no centralized policy from Salt Lake City in terms of how to determine bloodlines. In the absence of a central policy, it created, as you can imagine, a disparity across missions. One mission president would do it one way, and another mission president would do something different.

In Brazil, they were kind of trendsetters, if you will. They did what are called lineage lessons. The mission president instructed the missionaries, and the mission president I should say got approval from Salt Lake to do this lineage lesson. But it really was just mostly practiced in Brazil, rather than other places with African populations. But anyway, these lineage lessons stipulated that if missionaries were out proselytizing and they came across somebody who had African ancestry, who had a parent that they felt would be a prime candidate for the restriction. They were supposed to come to the door, knock on the door, recognize that they were under the ban and they would just say, "Can you tell us we're in the neighborhood; we are trying to find this general store or other church. Can you tell us where it is?"

If they weren't sure if this couple had African ancestry, then they would come in and ask questions about their genealogy, trying to determine through discussion if they had African roots. Sometimes they would even ask to look at their photo album. They were discrete about it. They weren't going to tell people this is what we are looking for, but this shows you how difficult the burden was in determining the bloodline. J. Reuben Clark recognized this as early as 1938 and expressed skepticism that the church could confer the priesthood on Brazilians without violating this policy.

At one point a little later on in the 1940s and '50s, J. Reuben Clark more than any other leader will work with a Mormon scientist named Alvin Mattson. He is a medical researcher. He's a medical doctor. He has got an M.D. Dr. Mattson will do his best to determine bloodlines scientifically. He is going to these conferences that deal with blood types and all of this stuff. He would write President Clark a note and say, "This is what I learned." I think we're getting close to determine bloodlines scientifically. Clearly that doesn't happen. It doesn't happen that way. But J. Reuben Clark is really, really interested in determining scientifically how to tell if somebody has African blood or not. So, he is working with Dr. Mattson. This will go on well into the 1950s.

Where, When, & Why Did the One-Drop Rule Originate?

GT: I know that there was a quote. In fact, I remember talking to Paul Reeve about this, and he said you've got to be careful with that, because it is not the best source, where Wilford Woodruff had written in his journal[10] that Brigham Young had said a man can't have one drop of African blood, although from what I understand now, that's not an exact quote. {Matt nods.} We need to be a little bit careful with that that reference.

But I know that you're a big U.S. history guy too, so there was a talk about the one-drop rule even with regards to slavery. Is that something that kind of morphed into the LDS Church and you couldn't have [more than] one drop of African blood in order to hold the priesthood as well?

Matt: Yes, after the American Civil War, there is this big push especially among people in the South to preserve bloodlines, racial purity really is what it is. After the Civil War, a number of states pass miscegenation laws preventing not just black people from marrying white people, but also Asians from marrying whites, and so forth, so it's not just blacks and whites. One of the purposes is to preserve the bloodlines, the purity of the bloodlines, so they pass these miscegenation laws.

They also make other moves, the eugenics movement will take off after the Civil War, trying to take people who have, as they put it, "inferior genes" from reproducing. Not surprisingly they'll target black people, not wanting them to reproduce, particularly if they have a low IQ and so forth, or if they have some kind of a—I guess they called it mental retardation in those days. We don't use that word

---

[10] See our interview at https://gospeltangents.com/2017/02/22/the-black-mormon-scandals/

today but that's what they were talking about. So, there is this eugenics idea that we don't want people with inferior genes to reproduce.

Also after the American Civil War, the courts, both state and national courts will codify this quarter, one-fourth negroid drop rule, which is to say that if you have one-quarter negroid blood in you then you are considered African-American. What is interesting about this is that depending on the state, these laws are very fluid in the early 20th century. I tell my students, we teach civil rights and we talk about this. In fact, we discuss the book Loving vs. Virginia, which is the Supreme Court case that strikes down these miscegenation laws, declares them unconstitutional. This is 1967.

But anyway, what's interesting is that in the early 20th century these miscegenation laws are very fluid. One state might say it's one-quarter. Another state might say it's one-eighth, or one-sixteenth. I joke with my students sometimes that on Monday, a black man can marry a white woman because they fit within the parameters of the law, but then they change the law on Wednesday and now it's no longer constitutional.

So, when we say race is a construct, this is really what this means, that the government is defining what these bloodlines are. The church is going to follow some of the most common of these court decisions, which is the one-quarter rule. That seemed to be the most prevalent around the turn of the century.

GT: So, just to make sure, if you're one-quarter black, then you can't marry a white?

Matt: That is correct.

GT: Ok.

Matt: And the church will follow those prevailing patterns, and so church leaders will tie it back to previous leaders. Ultimately, I don't know if Paul Reeve shared this with you, but ultimately a lot of leaders in the 20th century will tie it back to the prophet Joseph Smith. There is no evidence that the ban began with him. In fact in 2013 with the Race and Priesthood document,[11] it is the first document anywhere that the church produces where they lay the ban squarely at the feet of Brigham Young, and Joseph Fielding Smith and other church leaders had said that the ban began with Joseph Smith. That was sort of the common line, but the truth is there is no evidence for that. Scholars over the years have pointed that out.

Nonetheless these church presidents and other leaders thought that the ban began with the prophet Joseph Smith, but that's just not what the evidence bears. The Race and Priesthood document doesn't support that position. We know from the scholarship that Brigham Young is the person whose presidency creates the ban because there were several men who were ordained to the priesthood under Joseph Smith's tutelage.

GT: Now I think there still are some people who want to tie that to Joseph Smith. Have you seen anything like that, especially among anti-Mormon circles or anything?

Matt: You mean priesthood ordination to the prophet?

GT: Yes, to put it on Joseph instead of Brigham. Because it seems pretty clear from the priesthood essay that it seems like it started with Brigham Young, but a lot of people feel like we're throwing Brigham under the bus,

---

[11] See https://www.lds.org/topics/race-and-the-priesthood?lang=eng

and a lot of people would love to throw Joseph under the bus, especially critics of the church.

Matt: Well, I have to confess. I don't read anti-Mormon [literature,] so I don't know. I can't answer that question. I just don't read that stuff.

GT: Ok.

Matt: But it wouldn't surprise me if people tied it back to the prophet. I mean why wouldn't they? Church leaders have taught that for so many years. Even LDS manuals to this day still teach the ban, at least the manual I saw a year or two ago, tied the ban back to the prophet.

GT: To Joseph.

Matt: Yes.

GT: Oh, wow.

Matt: It's just a matter of cleaning up the manuals, printing a new edition. That's all it is.

GT: We've been using these manuals for 20 years. I think that it's time for an update, personally.

Matt: Yes, that's all it is. I don't think it represents, it's strange to say this, it doesn't represent the current views. It represents the views of 20 years ago when the manual was created.

GT: Right.

Matt: But the church has definitely evolved in its understanding of the ban with the prophet vs. Brigham Young.

GT: I should ask Paul this question, but I'm going to ask it to you since Paul is not here. I don't know how familiar you are with the work that Paul has done, but I know that Paul has said we need to be careful about using the Woodruff journal because in the journal it does say "one drop" in there. I believe this is in reference to Brigham Young's address in 1852. Paul says that when you actually look at the transcript—he's actually working on a documentary history for the Utah legislature of 1852. The words "one drop" does not exist in there. So, that seems like Wilford inserted that into the record when Brigham Young didn't actually say that.

But I guess my question is, even if you say that is a misquote from Wilford Woodruff, does it seem reasonable that even as early as 1852, Mormons were using this idea of one drop as a reason to deny blacks the priesthood?

Matt: Well, you know it is always an interesting question about when one leader says something, does it constitute church teaching, church direction, the doctrine of the church? Of course, with Brigham Young being the very powerful leader that he was, it's so different today in the way we create doctrine in the Mormon Church. The First Presidency and the Quorum of the Twelve will agree to it, vote on it, and prayerfully consider it. But in those days, when Brigham Young spoke, he spoke. From my reading, the one-quarter rule doesn't really emerge in the Mormon lexicon until after the 20th century.

GT: Oh, really.

Matt: This is when you start the—probably late 19th century, B.H. Roberts and certainly Joseph Fielding Smith and Bruce R. McConkie where they start to really hammer home this idea that if you have one-quarter drop in you, then you are disqualified from the priesthood. I see the evidence of that in the 20th century is overwhelming.

The question is, when does it start in the 19th century? Wilford Woodruff does say it in the 1850s. It certainly doesn't mean it is an accepted church teaching at that time. But for me the evidence really picks up, probably with B.H. Roberts around the turn of the century. I don't think any Mormon leader really questions this in the 20th century. In fact, I would argue that in 1852 they are still trying to work all this stuff out.

There is a nice piece of scholarship out there, one of the reasons for the ban is that Brigham Young is upset that one of the early black brethren were marrying into polygamy without permission. He was just revolted by that.

GT: Warner McCary.[12]

Matt: Warner McCary, yes. That's where we get some of the tough statements that Brigham Young makes about interracial unions and interracial sex and so forth. But anyway, this messiness is unfolding in the 19th century. It really becomes accepted in the 20th century. When Mormons start to talk about it, Joseph Fielding Smith and some other leaders, you can see a parallel with national trends after the Civil War. It's not surprising, at least in my view, that Americans are talking about the one-quarter negroid rule. Mormons are following this rule as well. So, that's what I would feel comfortable saying about the one-quarter rule. It's hard to know precisely when it precisely started, but it was certainly around the 20th century.

GT: Ok, so into the 20th century, you're saying that if a person had one-quarter black blood, basically a grandparent, right?

Matt: Correct.

---

[12] See our interview with Newell Bringhurst for more information on McCary at https://gospeltangents.com/2018/02/25/warner-mccary-real-native-genius/

GT: Then they could not be ordained.

Matt: Correct.

GT: So, do we have somebody that says, well my great-grandparent [is black], could they be ordained?

Matt: Well, it's interesting.

GT: Or is it a gray area?

Matt: It depends on who you ask. One of the things about this ban, and my work tries to point this out, this next book that I'm doing, I really want folks to see how this policy, this ban, and it's both a temple and a priesthood ban, how it plays out and affects real-life people, both people of color, black folks, white folks, and also church leaders too, some of whom can't reconcile the justness of Christ with this difficult teaching. Then there are some other leaders who have inherited it uncritically, and they don't really ask the hard questions: is this really something we ought to be doing? Why are we denying our black brothers and sisters these privileges?

Certainly, they read their scriptures into it. Mormon leaders are not unique in thinking that black folks are cursed from Cain, the biblical counter-figure. Then of course by the turn of the century, there is a new rationale for the priesthood ban, which is that they were less valiant in the pre-mortal existence. This is uniquely a Mormon thinking. But the whole curse thing is very Protestant in notion. It goes all the way back to the ancient world to be honest.

So anyway, Mormons inherit this Protestant dogma, and they just inherit it uncritically. They don't ask about it. If we can just jump ahead for a moment, one of the things that a junior apostle in 1978, Elder Haight, David B. Haight, he said something interesting. He said, "When we overturned the priesthood ban, none of us really asked, is this the right thing to do? We just inherited it from our predecessors, and we just continued it."

I thought that was a pretty revealing statement by Elder Haight. Gosh, maybe this wasn't the right thing to do. So, obviously President Kimball and Elder Haight was part of that process. Yes, a lot of these racial views will emerge from the larger American society. You will see truthfully, and I mean this respectfully, you'll read some of the leaders, Elder McConkie and his father-in-law, Joseph Fielding Smith, I mean it reads just like a southern Protestant clergyman when they are talking about segregation, civil rights, and so forth, and the Curse of Cain. Really in my view there is no distinction with some of the sermons, if you juxtapose them. So, Latter-day Saints again are not unique in some of these beliefs.

GT: Ok.

Did Pres. McKay Try to Rescind Ban in the 1954-55?

GT: Alright, well let's jump back into World War II again.

Matt: Yeah, alright.

GT: That was a nice side-trip into the 19th century there. So, tell us more. I guess it was in the 1940s or '50s when McKay went down to South Africa and overturned the [policy.]

Matt: Correct, 1952.

GT: '52. So, he was the new prophet in 1951.

Matt: He was. Yep.

GT: Take us through the '50s decade there. What are some of the important events there?

Matt: Well, what's interesting is President McKay. He had learned about the ban before this. He had been a missionary. I think Greg Prince talks about this in his excellent biography of President McKay.[13] But this is the first time that this new church president is really confronting this really difficult issue of determining who has this black ancestry. What happens is President McKay gets back from South Africa in the spring of 1952, or was it '53? It's one of the two.

GT: I'm not sure.

Matt: '52 or '53. Let me think about this for a minute. So, he gets back and he commissions a report. He wants to look into the matter if this ban ought to continue. He

---

[13] Can be purchased at https://amzn.to/2L2XtSw

wants to know in particular, is there scriptural justification for this ban? This is interesting because President McKay, as a counselor to George Albert Smith had signed that 1949 First Presidency statement[14] that you referenced a minute ago....

GT: Right.

Matt: ...as a counselor.

GT: Now let's talk about that '49 statement.

Matt: Yes, we can. So, as the church president, he signed that statement, and we can go into detail in a minute, but that statement makes it pretty clear that this is the doctrine of the church.

GT: And it uses the word "doctrine."

Matt: It uses the word doctrine.

GT: That is an important word.

Matt: Right. J. Reuben Clark writes the statement, and President McKay signs off on it. George Albert Smith is feeble by this point, and he is going to die a couple of years later, but anyway, President McKay, even though he signs that '49 statement, now he is the church president and he feels the weight of this policy on his own. When he gets back from South Africa, he convenes a meeting or a committee of apostles to look into it, and it is chaired by an apostle named Adam S. Bennion. Spencer W. Kimball is a junior apostle. He is on that committee as well.

---

[14] Can be found at http://signaturebookslibrary.org/neither-white-nor-black-appendix/

Interestingly enough, they reach to probably one of Mormonism's most beloved leaders outside of church leadership, an Institute [of Religion][15] teacher at the University of Utah named Lowell Bennion. Brother Bennion had been very vocal in a nice way, in a non-activist way. He was a very gentle man. I want to be clear about that. But anyway, he was very, very clear that he didn't think that the ban was justified in the scriptures. He was a very close friend with David O. McKay. In fact, outside of church leadership, he might have been second only to Stephen L. Richards, President McKay's counselor. Lowell Bennion might have been one of President McKay's closest counselors or advisors.

GT: Now Lowell Bennion, Adam Bennion. Is there a relationship there?

Matt: Yes, I am not sure what it is.

GT: But they are related somehow.

Matt: Yes. They are cousins I think.

GT: Ok.

Matt: I should look that up. Anyway, not surprising, Elder [Adam] Bennion, not surprising reaches out to his relative Lowell Bennion. Lowell Bennion, I should say by this point has made it very clear in private, he is not a crusader, and he didn't crusade in his classroom at the University of Utah Institute where he spent the bulk of his teaching career in the Church Education System, but people in his class knew that he didn't support the ban, but he left it at that.

---

[15] The LDS Church has set up Institutes of Religion at many colleges and universities in the United States to provide religious instruction to college students. The courses do not provide college credit, but LDS students are encouraged to take religious classes in addition to their college classes. LDS often refer to it simply as "Institute."

Anyway, he made his views known to President McKay, so McKay knew about them and it's not surprising that when McKay came back from South Africa and convenes this committee with Elders Bennion and Kimball, I'm not sure who else is on the committee, but I know it's those two. They ask Lowell Bennion to do some research for them, and he produces a position paper, and he says there is no scriptural justification for any of this stuff. So, Elder Bennion writes his report to President McKay and tells him that there is no scriptural justification for the priesthood ban. This is 1954 I should say.

So, President McKay contemplates lifting the ban, but he recognizes that it will cause hardship among the saints in the South. Keep in mind this is still segregated America. So, if he lifts this ban, it is going to create hardships among Latter-day Saints in the South. Also, there are some folks in the Quorum of Twelve who wouldn't support the lifting of the ban: Joseph Fielding Smith would be one of them. You know that he wasn't on that committee.

{GT chuckles}

Matt: Also, it is about the time of this report comes out that you may have heard that President McKay had a meeting with Sterling McMurrin, a philosopher at the University of Utah, a very liberal Latter-day Saint man. His grandfather was the Presiding Bishop of the church, so he had some deep roots in Mormon history. Anyway, he was always loyal to the church, McMurrin, in the sense that he wanted to defend it when he thought it needed to be defended, but he was very critical about the black issue. He asked President McKay about the ban just as this Bennion committee was formalizing its report and after they formed their report, Lowell Bennion had suggested that there was no scriptural justification for it, Elder

Bennion passed that along to President McKay, and President McKay told Sterling McMurrin, this non-practicing Latter-day Saint at the University of Utah, he said that the ban was not rooted in doctrine, but was a policy. That has been out there for a little bit, that statement.

GT: Right.

Matt: This is '54 when that statement comes out. It's not until '68 when it becomes known.

GT: So this is just five years after that First Presidency statement.

Matt: That is correct.

GT: So we go from a doctrine in '49 to a policy in '54.

Matt: That is correct. Yes, that is absolutely correct. Obviously, there is some differences of views in this kind of things, because Joseph Fielding Smith and Elder Mark E. Peterson, they think that it is rooted in scripture, it is rooted in doctrine, and President McKay is saying, no, it is policy. Then if it is policy of course, then it means it can be changed.

Just to finish the thought here, President McKay will invite a Canadian man named Hugh B. Brown, will call him as an apostle first. He is a member of the Assistants to the Quorum of Twelve.

GT: Which would probably be a Seventy today.

Matt nods: Which would probably be a Seventy today, and then I think it is 1953 he is called into the Quorum. In 1958[16] he is elevated to the First Presidency. Anyway,

---

[16] Matt misspoke. Brown was called as an apostle in 1958 and was elevated to the First Presidency at the death of J. Reuben Clark in 1961.

Hugh B. Brown had long been an opponent of the priesthood ban and didn't think there was any scriptural justification for it.

So, now you have got this Bennion report, you have got this very charismatic, influential new apostle Hugh B. Brown, and then you have got President McKay. Then you have got some of the other folks in the quorum who are very, I guess we would call them doctrinal hardliners. I mean this is what the scriptures say and if you know anything about Joseph Fielding Smith, you know that he was a hardliner.

GT: Well, he wrote a book that addressed the priesthood ban that I think we wouldn't be too proud of right now. Is that true?

Matt: Yes, he wrote a book in 1931, and it's a tough book. It is probably the most important book. I talk about this in my next book a lot, how influential that Joseph Fielding Smith was. He was called into the Quorum of Twelve in 1910 when he was in his early 30s. His father was a significant figure, his brother I think was in the Quorum of the Twelve, so he has got some deep stock in church leadership. Of course, Joseph Smith and Hyrum Smith, you know what they are to Joseph Fielding Smith.[17]

He writes a book in 1931 and he outlines in the three chapters his views about the ban. He ties it back to Joseph Smith. He, of course, talks about the Old Testament scriptures of the Curse of Cain and Ham and all of that. It's that book that really, really defines the tone for church

---

[17] Joseph Fielding Smith eventually became 10th LDS Church president. His father was Joseph F. Smith who was 6th LDS Church president, and his grandfather was Hyrum Smith, brother of founder Joseph Smith. Hyrum served as Assistant President to the Church and was killed with Joseph Smith when a mob stormed the Carthage Jail June 27, 1844 in Carthage, Illinois.

leadership by the mid part of the 20th century. Because
when Latter-day Saints, and even people not of the faith
are writing into the First Presidency asking about the ban,
the General Authorities are sending back chapters 15 and
16 of Joseph Fielding Smith's book. They will say, read
these chapters. It explains everything. So, it becomes the
go-to guide. It goes through several reprint editions. It
comes out in 1931, and I don't think it was removed from
print until 1984.

GT: Wow, 50 years.

Matt: The book is controversial, because of the curse and
all of that stuff.

GT: What was the name of the book?

Matt: Let's see. What is the name of the book? You would
ask me, put me on the spot.

GT: That's alright.

Matt: It will come to me in three minutes and I will blurt it
out!

GT: I am trying to remember. Is it something about Perfection?

Matt: Yes, it has Perfection in the title.[18] I am tempted to
look it up on my phone. {both chuckle} Yes, it's funny how
I remember the date it was published in 1931 and I can't
remember the title of the book. My kids would joke that I
know the plotline of the move but I can't remember the
movie.

{GT chuckles}

---

[18] The book is called *The Way to Perfection*. Used copies can be found at
https://amzn.to/2Ld0K1D

Matt: But anyway, it's this book. It comes out in 1931 and what is interesting about this book is, I'm told by a BYU professor who has done a lot of research in Brazil, Mark Grover is his name, a really wonderful man. Mark told me that when they published Joseph Fielding Smith's book in Brazil, they left out chapters 15 and 16.

GT chuckles: Really?

Matt: Yes, because it's kind of tough stuff.

GT: Yeah.

Matt: This same book is one of the books that influences his son-in-law when he writes his classic book, *Mormon Doctrine*.[19]

GT: Which would be Bruce R. McConkie.

Matt: Which would be Bruce R. McConkie, yes. So, anyway, that's what is going on in the 1950s. Also, I should say a word. It's really interesting. A lot of people, there is a lot of students in the Church Education System and also at BYU. This is the 1950s. The Civil Rights Movement hasn't quite taken off yet, at least as we know it today from the '60s. We see a groundswell of racial equality that will emerge from the *Brown vs. the Board [of Education] decision* in 1954[20]. Then you get the murder of Emmitt Till,[21] Rosa Parks.[22] But the church leaders will

---

[19] Can be purchased at https://amzn.to/2IRH2du

[20] This was a landmark U.S. Supreme Court decision that outlawed segregation of schools based on race. For more info, see
https://en.wikipedia.org/wiki/Brown_v._Board_of_Education

[21] Emmett Till was a 14-year-old African-American who was lynched in Mississippi in 1955, after a white woman said she was offended by him in her family's grocery store. The brutality of his murder and the fact that his killers were acquitted drew attention to the long history of violent persecution of African Americans in the United States. For more info, see

start to talk about it in earnest. What do we do about the Brown decision where we de-segregate schools? The church is worried about this because if you break down de-segregation, and you allow blacks and whites to go to school together, to work together, of course that creates a familiarity, an intimacy. Ultimately, they will start to be friends. They will start to date, and then eventually marry. That is really what they are worried about.

This is why they are opposed to the Brown decision. Most leaders are opposed to the *Brown vs. Board* decision. This is why they are opposed initially to civil rights, because if you break down those racial barriers, it will lead to miscegenation. They just don't think that is what God wants. So anyway, you do start to see these things percolating up.

I'm getting ahead of myself. Back at BYU, some of these CES students start to write to church leaders, these are college students now, asking, why are we denying black people these privileges? There are BYU faculty who create this underground, if you will, some of whom are in the Religious Education department, and they are starting to question the ban, not publicly, but privately. They are scratching their heads: "I don't see this in the scriptures. What is going on?"

One young woman writes in 1952 to President McKay and says, "Can you tell me why we can't give black people the

---

[22] Rosa Parks refused to obey bus driver's order to give up her seat in the "colored section" to a white passenger, after the whites-only section was filled in Montgomery, Alabama. This led to the Montgomery bus boycott and was a major civil rights action. For more info, see https://en.wikipedia.org/wiki/Rosa_Parks

priesthood? Help me out with my research. I am going to do a research paper for my English class."

President McKay writes Ernest Wilkinson a letter, Xeroxes the letter from the student so he had background knowledge. He said, "Would you please reach out to her and tell her that we are not interested in researching things of this nature?"

GT: Really?

Matt: Yes.

GT: Wow.

Matt: Ernest Wilkinson, the BYU president, broke the news to this young woman from Orem, Utah.

GT: Wow.

Matt: Yes, 1952. So, you see this a lot in the '50s. It's forcing the brethren to really think about what their views are, especially as the national current trends going on with civil rights. It puts the church in a really tough position, because the winds are blowing one way and the church is standing firm, thinking that they have inherited this doctrine from the prophet Joseph Smith that they ought not to give black people the priesthood and temple privileges.

GT: Hmmm, very interesting.

Matt: Yes.

Hugh B. Brown's Attempt to End Ban in 1962!

GT: Let's jump into the '60s then, I guess. Let's talk a little bit about the Civil Rights Era. We can talk a little bit about President Benson. Take us there.

Matt: Ok, alright. So, that was the '50s with the Brown decision, and some rumblings in the CES system with students thinking about this. I think nationally this racial story gets really highlighted when George Romney decides to run for president. This is really interesting. He is the governor of a state that has a heavy African-American population.

Now think about that for a moment. Your church doesn't grant priesthood rights to black people, and you are running in a campaign for governor, and you are having to convince people that you are not a racist or that somehow if you are elected you won't listen to their needs and create public policy that will benefit their lives.

When George Romney is governor, when it is known that he is considering a run for the presidency, it is pretty interesting because a lot of the news media are writing about the LDS Church priesthood ban, and that Governor Romney may be a racist because his church is racist. It's pretty tough stuff, and George Romney will say something interesting. He will say, "If you want to know my views on race, look at my record when I was the governor. Look at what I did with civil rights."

So, he cleverly sidesteps his church's racial teachings and puts the spotlight on him, which is truthfully probably what he probably should have done and what he did. But

nonetheless the media will continue to hammer this issue.
Spencer W. Kimball in particular, he writes letters to
various people. He writes in his journal, and he says, "The
media is just killing us with George Romney. Is that all
they ever want to talk about is the negro issue?"

So, they are very sensitive to this. There are other
Mormons like Sterling McMurrin who are critical too
nationally. They are getting a lot of national attention and
Elder Kimball is just going crazy over this.

GT: Spencer Kimball.

Matt: Spencer Kimball, then Elder Kimball.

GT: Really? Ok.

Matt: Yes, he said, "I wish the Sterling McMurrins of the
world would leave us alone," he writes.

GT: Really, that's interesting.

Matt: Yes. He also throws in another man we haven't
talked about yet. He says the "Sterling McMurrins" and
"Lowry Nelsons" of the world would "leave us alone."
Lowry Nelson is the man that is responsible for that 1949
First Presidency statement. Just a quick bio on him.

Born in Utah, went to school at BYU for a while. I think he
graduated from BYU,[23] as an undergrad. He went to
graduate school at I think the University of Wisconsin in
sociology. So, he is a Utah native. He taught at Utah
State for a while and he spent the majority of his career,
he spent some time in Florida. The majority of his career

---

[23] Lowry Nelson graduated from Utah State Agriculatural College in 1916, which
became Utah State University. See
http://archiveswest.orbiscascade.org/ark:/80444/xv80172

was at the University of Minnesota. He was a fairly prominent sociologist. He had a friend named Heber Meeks who was the president of the Cuban Mission. The brethren had asked Meeks to go open up this Cuban mission. This would have been in the mid-1940s. Meeks knew Lowry Nelson. They both grew up together.

Recognizing that Lowry Nelson had spent time in Cuba as part of his profession, his field research, he decided to reach out to Nelson and ask him about Cuba and the racial population there because Nelson had lived there for a while. Lowry Nelson wrote back and just said, "I don't think you can determine who has got negroid blood, and you shouldn't even try! That's just immoral!"

Nelson said something that is probably less than candid. He said, "That was the first time I knew that the church felt this way about this."

Come on Lowry. You grew up in the church. So, Lowry Nelson writes the First Presidency after he exchanged correspondence with his good friend Heber Meeks. He said, "Is it true that you are trying to establish a mission in Cuba, and just focus on the white population there and not the colored, the brown population? Is that true?"

The First Presidency wrote him back a series of letters. They said, "Yes that is true, and we don't understand why God wants this ban, but this is the way it is. Who are you to determine what God should do?"

Nelson was really upset with the response, thinking that it was just a policy that could be changed. But the brethren dug their heels in and sort of exacerbated the problem. When they wrote back to Lowry Nelson, it was the first time where the First Presidency goes on record, and they sign the letter. It is interesting. They all sign these letters back and forth, all three of them: George Albert Smith, J. Reuben Clark, and David O. McKay. Clearly, they are trying to make a statement about the church's racial teachings, at least by the mid-20th century.

What is interesting is he shares these letters on the underground with people. He sends them to Juanita Brooks.[24] He sends them to George Boyd who is the Institute person. He sends them to all of these Institute people that he felt like he had a liberal kinship with, and they write him back. "Oh my goodness. I didn't know the brethren felt this way, that they felt this strongly about it."

They were disappointed. So, there was this underground where the Lowry Nelson correspondence with the First Presidency, there is, I don't know, a dozen letters maybe total. Anyway, they get shipped around everywhere among this "Mormon underground," so people are getting a firsthand look at what the leadership are thinking about this difficult issue.

President McKay is struggling with it. He signs his name to the letter. J. Reuben Clark wrote it, I mentioned, but President McKay signs his name to the letter and President McKay will have a very difficult time with this. He will maintain the status quo, but through the 1960s when civil rights are coming, maybe I should get to that point.

But during the Civil Rights Era, George Romney is contemplating a presidential run, the NAACP in Utah, the Salt Lake City chapter, they are threatening to march on Salt Lake City at Temple Square during Conference for two reasons: because the church hasn't agreed to support a national civil rights bill that had been working its way

---

[24] Juanita Brooks wrote the first scholarly book exposing Mormon involvement in the Mountain Meadows Massacre. See https://amzn.to/2LcbRrG

through congress in the summer of 1963. So, the NAACP were upset that the church leadership—they couldn't understand why they can't you support a civil rights bill. We understand your priesthood ban, but why not the civil rights bill? This just seems like the humane thing to do.

Then the other thing was, they were upset that the church, or the state of Utah had some very draconian laws that dealt with race. There's nothing to protect employment discrimination against black people. They were upset about that, so the state of Utah didn't practice what they call—didn't have a law that would protect fair practices in hiring, as they called it. So, you could discriminate based on your race, in other words.

So, they were really putting pressure on the church both at the state and national levels. In that context, Hugh B. Brown and N. Eldon Tanner, both of whom were in the First Presidency by the early '60s. Henry Moyle had died and J. Reuben Clark had died just a couple of years earlier. So, these two men in the First Presidency met with the NAACP and they said, "Let's strike a deal. If we agree to read a statement in General Conference," this is October of 1963, just as all of this stuff is percolating. "If we agree to read a statement in General Conference, offering support for civil rights, would you cancel the protest?"

Johnnie Driver then leader of the NAACP at the time agreed to do it. So, what is interesting is the majority of the Twelve didn't support Civil Rights, but Hugh Brown did. Nathan Tanner did too. So, they go to President McKay and said, "Look, this is the deal we have reached. Are you ok with this?"

President McKay is a product of his generation, and he wasn't in favor of civil rights because he feared interracial marriage. That was his modus operandi. President McKay didn't want the bad publicity from the march distracting from General Conference. Reluctantly, he gives the green light to President Brown to read a statement in the October 1963 General Conference session.

What is interesting though, is he said to President Brown, he said, "When you read the statement, make sure it is part is part of your larger your talk. We don't want to give the impression this is coming from the First Presidency."

Hugh B. Brown, funny guy, clever guy, completely ignored the boss's wishes. He had great affection for President McKay. But anyway, at this point, he ignored President McKay. He begins his talk. He says, "I have a statement I wish to read." So, he gives the impression that it is supported by the First Presidency, which is not what President McKay wanted him to do!

"Incorporate it into your talk."

So, he reads this statement, it's like two paragraphs, and then he pretty much says, "Now I'm going to begin my talk." {Both chuckle}

What is interesting, apostle Kimball, Elder Kimball will write in his journal, "Huh! The church supports civil rights. Who knew?"

GT chuckles: Really?

Matt: So he said, I mean I'm being a little flippant, but Elder Kimball writes that "President Brown read a statement on civil rights today in General Conference giving the church position."

GT chuckles: Really? Giving the Church position, which McKay specifically didn't want him to do.

Matt: Right. You can downplay it because of all the racial tension and all of that stuff. Quite frankly, a number of them, as I said before, didn't believe in civil rights at the time. So, anyway, Hugh B. Brown was front and center in church leadership trying to get the brethren to overturn the ban. He is working behind the scenes. He is doing the best that he can, but it is very, very challenging for him. In 1962 he will have a private meeting with Lowell Bennion, whom we have already talked about who didn't support the ban and told President McKay in private. So, it was no secret that President McKay knew where Brother Bennion stood. Anyway, in March of 1962, Hugh B. Brown tells Lowell Bennion, "We're going to lift the ban here next month. Make sure you come to [General] Conference."[25]

GT: '62?!

Matt: This is March of '62.

GT: Wow.

Matt: "Come to Conference next month. We're going to lift the ban."

The prediction of course is in April of '62, we're going to have this big announcement at General Conference. "We have been studying this issue, and there is nothing more difficult for the church," Brown tells Bennion, "than this issue, and we're going to fix it."

---

[25] LDS leaders hold a twice annual conference where members hear the prophet, apostles, Seventies, young men, your women, and Primary (children's) leaders speak every April and October. LDS members often refer to the meetings as simply "Conference." In the 1960s, General Conference lasted 3 days, but was shorted to two days in 1977. See
https://en.wikipedia.org/wiki/General_Conference_(LDS_Church)

So, I can only imagine Bennion showing up and nothing happens! Anyway, we don't know a lot of the details behind the scenes, but clearly it is not lifted. About six weeks after the conference in 1962, Joseph Fielding Smith writes something in the Church News. "We're not lifting this ban."

I mean he's pretty clear about it. As a scholar I read this, there is a lot of discussion about it, and President Brown likes to talk. I should tell you too, he told the *New York Times* reporter the same thing as Bennion. "We are going to lift this ban."

GT: In '62.

Matt: In '62, yes.

GT: Wow.

Matt: So this is now public and Elder Smith, President Smith, I guess he was president of the Quorum of Twelve at that point, President Smith wants to reaffirm to the saints who read the *New York Times* that this isn't going to happen. So anyway, in 1963, a whole year later President Brown says the same thing again to Wallace Turner of the *New York Times*: "We're going to lift the ban."

This time it creates a lot of hardship because Elder Smith is upset about this. He is talking publicly. These are private matters. I will let you speculate why he is talking to the media. This is really interesting. Can you imagine today? Let's pause for a moment. The First Presidency counselor is talking to the media about some big policy change, before it has been signed off or approved by the brethren. I mean, oh my goodness!

So, President Brown, we can only imagine he is trying to put external pressure on the church. Really, that is one of the logical conclusions. So, he talks to the reporter, and there is a man, I can't remember the guy's name, somebody from Salt Lake is there at the interview, and he is just aghast when he hears President Brown talking. He is taking notes. He goes back to Salt Lake, and he tells President McKay, "Did you know that President Brown gave an interview a couple fo days ago. I was there. He said we're going to lift the ban. I've got the notes!"

GT: Wow.

Matt: Poor President Brown, he said he was misquoted. He was in a hardship. He wasn't misquoted. Wallace Turner had the transcript, plus the other guy was there from Salt Lake. President Brown in his heart of hearts just felt very strongly that the ban wasn't scriptural and wasn't borne out of divine revelation. It was just a policy that they had inherited that needed to be overturned.

As the Civil Rights movement moved along, I will just make this our last comment here about this, by the late 1960s, the church was under tremendous pressure to lift the priesthood ban, both inside and outside the church. Sterling McMurrin is giving these public addresses to the NAACP that dozens of newspaper outlets are publishing. He is really presenting the church in an unflattering light.

You've got high a profile Mormon official in the Jack Kennedy administration, also the Lyndon Johnson administration. He's a holdover into Lyndon Johnson, a guy named Stuart Udall, and he goes public. You've got Stewart Udall and Sterling McMurrin, Secretary of the Interior. He goes public with his views about the ban, which is very interesting. So, you've got Stewart Udall, and then Sterling McMurrin, who was also in the Kennedy administration briefly. He was the Secretary of Education to Kennedy, and he realized government politics wasn't for him, so he went back to Salt Lake to be a professor. But nonetheless, you had these two cabinet guys, and very prominent Mormons, expressing public disapproval for the ban.

Almost Famous: 1969 Black Ordination Nixed by Lee

Matt: By 1968, I'm sure you know about this, that dozens of athletic teams will start to protest BYU. They are very clear about this. We are really protesting BYU athletics, but it's the church racial policies that we are after. So, they are using BYU to get to the church.

In the midst of all of this, Hugh B. Brown will try yet another time to get this ban reversed. In September of 1969, in the midst of some very, very heavy protesting and very unflattering news coverage, President Brown will visit with two of David O. McKay's sons and say, "Can you help me? We have got to do something about this. Because if we don't get this ban lifted, because if we don't get this ban lifted before your father dies," keep in mind that President McKay is in his 90s at this point. He has got moments of lucidity and moments where he is not lucid; good days and bad days. "But if we don't get this ban lifted when he is alive, then your father's successor and his successor's successor won't lift it," meaning Joseph Fielding Smith and Harold B. Lee, both of whom are doctrinal hardliners.

So, in September of 1969 during the midst of some heavy, heavy protesting at BYU, the two McKay sons and President McKay go to the Hotel Utah[26] where President McKay now lives and he was convalescing, and there is a lot of details I

---

[26] The Hotel Utah, completed in 1911, was an LDS Church owned hotel across the street from the Salt Lake Temple and was the home of several LDS Church presidents. The hotel ceased operations in 1987, the building was remodeled and renamed the Joseph Smith Memorial Building in 1993. The church later bought the street between the buildings, and turned the street into a park.

am leaving out, but anyway, there is a book that had been published by a Mormon graduate student at Cornell named Stephen Taggart. Taggart's book, we think that is it superficial today, and it is. It is not very deeply researched, but he argues that the policy was borne out of Joseph Smith's era, essentially out of 19th century conditions of slavery. There was nothing divine about it. That's what he argued.

Anyway, the McKay sons and Brown, when Taggart's thesis comes out, they will use Taggart's research and say, "Look. This is just a policy. This is a policy, it is not a doctrine. So, if it is just a policy, President McKay, then we can overturn this." President McKay agrees to ordain a black man named Monroe Fleming, a loyal member at the Hotel Utah. This is in September of 1969.

GT: Wow.

Matt: Yes, yes. So, he agrees to ordain Monroe Fleming to the priesthood. It is interesting, the document that I have that talks about this. It just says Monroe Fleming. It doesn't say all persons of African ancestry. But you can only imagine that if you allow Monroe Fleming the priesthood, based upon his worthiness of course, then that means that other worthy black members of the church can now hold the priesthood. That's how I interpret that.

So, anyway, President McKay, who had been badgered by Brown for years to do this, and not just Brown but others as well, he had been badgered. He resisted it for a lot of reasons. Particularly thinking that it might harm the church in the South, and also Joseph Fielding Smith and Harold B. Lee, who had very strong feelings about the ban. He didn't want to create a hardship with members of the quorum. So, he agrees to do it, and when Harold B. Lee and Joseph Fielding Smith, mostly Harold B. Lee, because Joseph Fielding Smith is now in his 90s, and his health is getting the best of him. But when Harold B. Lee finds out about it, he puts an end to it and says, "This is not something that we can do, and if we do it, it has to have buy-in from the Quorum of the Twelve, the full quorum."

So, President McKay, and I'm going to paraphrase, he says, "I'm too old to fight him. I'm not going to do it. We will let President Lee worry about this problem." That's what he says, this "problem."

Keep in mind, Harold Lee is now in his early 70s. He is not the next in line for the presidency but is after Joseph Fielding Smith. It was longed believed that President Smith wouldn't be the church president for very long based on his age. So, they thought in Harold Lee they would have another David O. who would lead the church for 20-plus years. Obviously, it didn't happen that way. He was only church president for 18 months before an untimely illness takes him.

But anyway, everyone thought in leadership that Harold B. Lee would be a church president for many years, and so let Elder Lee worry about this problem, President McKay thinks. So, what happens is, Brown, as you can imagine, is distraught, because this is the time to lift the ban, but "I need President McKay to do this," but he doesn't want to fight President Lee. So anyway, President Brown goes back to President McKay and he said, "If I can get each of the members of the Twelve to support this," remember this is a policy according to Brown, not a doctrine, and it doesn't require some divine revelation according to Brown. "President McKay, if I can get the majority of the Twelve to buy-in, would you support this?"

McKay said, "I will support this if you can get a majority of the Twelve to buy-in."

So, strategically, when Alvin Dyer who is now in the First Presidency, and when Harold B. Lee are out of town on church business, President Brown will meet with the majority of the Twelve to get their support. They agree to overturn the ban. This is in November of 1969, at the same time that the Western Athletic Conference (WAC), they are scheduled to hold a vote to kick BYU out of the conference. This is the stuff going on behind the scenes.

GT chuckles: There is a lot going on, because we haven't even hit Benson yet.

Matt: What is instructive here is so many Latter-day Saint scholars have told the BYU athletic protests, but they are missing the other component which is the stuff going on behind the scenes in church leadership. I don't think you can untie the two. They are really inextricably linked.

That's another thing. President Brown wants to lift the ban to get the athletic protests off their back. In November of '69 he tells Kenneth Pitzer the Stanford President. He calls him up. He said, "This is Hugh Brown of the Church of Jesus Christ of Latter-day Saints. I just want you to know, we are going to lift the ban."

GT: He calls the Stanford University president.

Matt: Yes, he calls the Stanford president and tells him we are going to lift the ban, and even writes him a letter.

GT: The reason why is because Stanford had just cancelled some sort of a series.

Matt: Correct.

GT: Was it football or basketball? Do you remember?

Matt: Basketball, I think it was basketball. It was that fall, they cancelled their contract with BYU basketball. I think those were the days when Stanford and BYU were both in the WAC.

GT: I think Stanford was in the Pac-8.[27]

Matt: Ok.

GT: BYU was in the WAC. Stanford was in the Pac-8.

Matt: You are right. They had a contract to play each other out of conference, I think is what it was.

GT: Yes, right.

Matt: Anyway, so he tells Pitzer this. President Brown, he has been one to talk to the public before, and he also gives an interview with a couple of news outlets too: "We're going to lift the ban." This is November of '69. Anyway, he gets the apostles to buy into it, and when Elder Lee comes back from his church assignment and he realizes what Brown has done, he is furious, as you can imagine. He feels like it is a slight to his authority. It is done behind closed doors, without his input. "How could you do this?" Elder Lee goes to each of the apostles who agreed to support President Brown and he convinces them to change their support, and they do.

Spencer W. Kimball, who is going to be the president of the Quorum of Twelve one day under Harold B. Lee's leadership goes to President Brown. He is sobbing. He is

---

[27] In 1978, the conference added Arizona State and Arizona to become the Pac-10 Conference. In 2010, the conference added Utah and Colorado to become the Pac-12 Conference.

weeping, and he said, "I know you are right. We need to lift the ban, but I fear Brother Lee." By that he meant he was going to have to work under Brother Lee and he didn't want to create any sort of antagonism between these two men in their positions of leadership. So, he sobs to President Brown and says, "I have to change my vote to support him."

So, with all of that turmoil in the fall of 1969, and with President Brown and the majority of the Quorum of Twelve agreeing to lift the ban in 1969, Elder Lee wants to put a stop to that, and he recommends that they produce a second First Presidency statement in December of 1969; the first being in 1949, twenty years earlier with Lowry Nelson and George Albert Smith.

Well this second First Presidency statement reaffirms the ban, and they want the First Presidency to sign off on it. It is interesting. They want the guy who is trying to overturn the ban to sign his name to it: Hugh B. Brown. Brown reads the draft, and said, "I can't sign this." He is weeping as he reads it.

Harold Lee, who is a very dominant man, and a very incredibly skilled and able church administrator, but not known for his compassionate side. He is a very volatile personality his biographer concedes, which is his son-in-law,[28] a volatile personality. So, Harold Lee wants to form this committee to put this statement together.

He puts on the committee a guy named G. Homer Durham who is the president of Arizona State University. He is a political scientist. He would later be called as a general authority and be the managing director over the Church

---

[28] The book is called *Harold B. Lee: Prophet and Seer*, by L. Brent Goates, published by Bookcraft, 1985. It is found at https://amzn.to/2lzQLWn

Historical Department. This is in the late '70s. But in 1969, he was an academic serving as the president of ASU[29] in Tempe. So, they asked him to do it, and I guess the reason why they asked them is Gordon Hinckley is also on the committee and he and Hinckley were missionary companions as I recall. I think probably Elder Hinckley at the time wanted to have his good friend and his academic friend sit on the committee.

Also, a young Neal Maxwell was on the committee, and so they asked G. Homer Durham, Gordon Hinckley and Neal Maxwell to each produce drafts. I think Harold Lee presented a draft too, I think. Maybe he didn't. I don't recall. But anyway, there are three different drafts, and Elder Gordon B. Hinckley, his task is to meld the three drafts together. That was his assignment that Lee had given him. He said, "It was one of the most difficult assignments I have had in church leadership, creating this very difficult draft to produce a statement that we were still going to support this ban."

This final draft, when they amalgamate all of the different drafts, it's done, they want Brown to sign it. He reads it and weeps. There is no statement of civil rights, and he is just crestfallen. He tells Lee, "I'll sign this under one condition. If you put the civil rights back in there."

We already talked about it in 1963 ar Conference, and so Elder Lee agrees to put civil rights statement in there, and the story goes, from the Brown family, this is his own family who recount the story that Hugh B. Brown signs the document, weeping as he does so, because he doesn't support it. The other signature was N. Eldon Tanner. President McKay was too sick. This is December of 1969,

---

and President McKay will die in January of '70, so he is on his last legs. So, the two First Presidency counselors will sign the document and that is the context behind that second document in 1969 is all the stuff going on with BYU and behind the scenes with President Brown and President McKay.

Matt: Yes, so I'll just say a quick thought on that. That was the first time in any document that I have seen where the church moves to a "we don't know" position, which becomes sort of a quasi-official line for the next two or three decades after 1970, which is really interesting because before that, when you are Joseph Fielding Smith writing the books you write, and *Mormon Doctrine*, to say "we don't know" when you read those books, they know.

Really that line, it's a throwaway line in my view. It is based on a response to the Civil Rights Movement when people ask: "Why can't your church give black people priesthood rights?"

"Well, we don't know."

That's the response. In 1968 during the midst of a lot of the protesting at BYU, the First Presidency, there's a meeting they have. President McKay is there, Hugh B. Brown is there, N. Eldon Tanner, Alvin Dyer, and Joseph Fielding Smith. You recall that there were several counselors with President McKay in his later years, anyway they were all there, and I think it was President McKay who said, "When people ask us about the priesthood ban, we shouldn't talk about the Curse of Cain or anything like that. We should say to people, 'we don't know,' and keep our utterances very simple and positive towards black people/negro people, as he said."

So, President McKay, in a moment of lucidity is recognizing the challenges of a priesthood ban and telling black people they are cursed in the midst of the Civil Rights Movement. It's just not a good selling point.

GT: No.

Matt: So, he recognizes that the public relations dictate just keep the expressions simple and praiseworthy. That's the context in which they create the "we don't know" statement. They are trying to remove some of these justifications that got them into hot water. They still believe it of course, but yet that's now the new line that we don't know.

Really, for me as a scholar reading this stuff, it just really speaks to the challenges of having to deal with a very interesting issue. Also, it speaks to the idea that the brethren interpret the scriptures differently. I mean Hugh B. Brown clearly did not read the Old Testament the same way that Bruce R. McConkie or Joseph Fielding Smith read it. Even President McKay, I've looked at his writings and I don't think I've ever seen anything in his writings, and I've read a lot of his private writings too, where he ever said that black people were cursed.

GT: McKay never said that black people were cursed?

Matt: Yes, not that I can think of. He does refer to the Book of Abraham, and the less valiant position. That's the scriptural prooftext[30] that Latter-day Saints would typically

---

[30] Prooftexting is the practice of using decontextualised quotations from a document (often, but not always, a book of the Bible) to establish a proposition rhetorically through an appeal to authority. Critics of the technique note that

use to talk about the pre-mortal existence, so he does talk about that, but I can't recall an instance where he says, "Yes, black people are bore the mark of a divine curse." I don't think he believed it.

GT: Hmmm, that's interesting.

Matt: Yes.

GT: Now, when we look at it from '49 to '69, do you view that as progress from in 1949, it's a doctrine of God, and then in 1969, "Well we don't know." Would you view that as progress?

Matt: Well, I don't know about progress. That's a heavy word. Progress is Spencer W. Kimball, and the revelation of 1978. That's progress.

I would see this as something that is clearly evolving. Their racial views are evolving. What is interesting is you may have heard of James R. Clark. He is a BYU religion professor, and he is a distant relative of J. Reuben Clark. You have probably seen, what's the title of it? *Messages of the First Presidency*. It's a [six] volume book[31] that starts in 1965. I think the last edition is published in '75.

GT: Ok.

Matt: Anyway, I'm sure that you have run into it over the years. It was popular back in the day. Anyway, it is basically [six] volumes of LDS First Presidency messages, and he had to get special permission from the brethren in Salt Lake to publish these books. I think Bookcraft did it, as I recall.

---

often the document, when read as a whole, may not in fact support the proposition. See https://www.mormonmatters.org/proof-texting-for-fun-and-prophet/
[31] See https://amzn.to/2Lhr0le

So, as he was getting permission, everybody pointed him to the Church Historian, which was Joseph Fielding Smith at the time. He went into President Smith's office in Salt Lake City, and told him what he was doing. He knew who he was, a BYU religion professor. It was really interesting. President Smith said, "I give you my blessing. I will let you publish those things, but there is a couple that you shouldn't put in there." The 1949 First Presidency statement was one of them.

GT: Oh really?

Matt: Yes, and I think he mentioned something, there was one on polygamy. It was some statement I think he wanted to include on plural marriage that he wanted him to shy away from. But what was interesting is that tells me that the brethren were very conscious of what was going in the 1960s. They had used that '49 First Presidency statement in mission sermons. You can see different general authorities visiting missions and giving this statement. BYU religion professors were handing the '49 statement out to their students, so clearly it was the prevailing thought of the day. But by the later part of the '60s when the Civil Rights Movement kicks into high gear, I can't find any evidence that people are using this '49 statement.

By '65 when Clark goes to Joseph Fielding Smith and asks for permission, and he says, don't use that statement. So, President Smith, I think he is thinking about the optics of it all. By '69 with all of the context that we just talked about with BYU and the Brown stuff behind the scenes, that becomes the "we don't know" line to keep us off the hot seat.

Because one of the things that you learn when you go through the '60s and look at the brethren and their writings, you look at the *Church News*, public relations events when they open up a new temple, for example the Washington, D.C. Temple, the press is there. They get so tired of being asked about the Negro policy. Everywhere they go, in my humble opinion, from the 1960s on, it seems like everywhere they are at in public where the media are there, the first thing they want to know is not about that beautiful temple that we just created, they want to know about the negro ban and when are you going to lift it?

If you read their writings, I mean you can imagine. This is burdensome. They have a vision to share the gospel, to run the church, to fulfill the mission of the church, and these pesky journalists just want to know about the ban. It's hard to tell them about the ban, especially if you have these Protestant notions that black people are cursed. It is something they don't understand or they don't accept, much less say they are less valiant in the pre-mortal life. I mean this is very Mormon language here. How do you explain that to somebody? Well, you don't want to explain it to somebody.

So, they get so tired of answering. Finally, at one point when Harold B. Lee was sworn in as church president, he was asked it at his inauguration, first thing! When are you going to lift the ban?

President Lee was ready for it. These things are not surprising to them. "When are you going to lift the ban?"

He says, I'm going to paraphrase, "Well, you know, I don't even know why people like you ask me this question, because you're not even a member of my faith, and what difference does it make to you?" {both chuckle} I am being really crass about it but that is really what he is saying.

GT: Yes.

Matt: What difference does it make? It doesn't affect you. But anyway, Spencer Kimball, when he is the new church president, he is faced with the same thing. It really just bothers them.

How Kimball Persuaded Apostles to Agree on Lifting the Ban

GT: Alright, I just wanted to follow up on this Monroe Fleming. That kind of blew my mind a little bit. The one thing that I wanted to ask was when McKay was going to ordain him, I assume to the priesthood, whether it was Aaronic or Melchizedek, I guess it doesn't matter, but was that going to be a big announcement, and then, hey this is the first guy, and we are just going to do this for everybody? Or was this just, "You know what. You're a good guy and we're going to do this for you and you are the exception." What was the thought process there?

Matt: Well, the evidence isn't clear. It was just that we are going to ordain a loyal negro at the Hotel Utah. In fact, it doesn't even say Monroe Fleming's name in the document. But the "loyal negro" at the Hotel Utah is Monroe Fleming. He had been working there for years. Church leaders all knew him. Of course, it is a church-owned property. He was a very faithful member. I think he joins in the early '50s, so clearly he is a pioneer in the church. He comes of age in the church before the priesthood revelation, so he understands the restriction. But it is not clear if there is going to be an announcement; it's just that "We are going to ordain this loyal negro man." That's all it is. I think Hugh B. Brown mentions Monroe Fleming in a different document, but the McKay document that I have, it's just "a loyal negro member at the Hotel Utah."

GT: Wow. So, was he upset when this didn't happen? Do we have his reaction?

Matt: Oh, I wish we knew. I wish we knew. I can say a couple of things that over the years there were some newspaper reports when the revelation came out that they interviewed some prominent black LDS men, and Monroe Fleming is one of them. If you look at the *Salt Lake Tribune*, the *Deseret News* from the summer of '78 when the priesthood revelation came out, they would interview these black Latter-day Saints and ask about the ban. Monroe Fleming is there. [He said,] "I waited patiently. I was so happy to have the priesthood," and this sort of thing.

But he wasn't patient. He is not happy. He was working behind the scenes. He is writing scholars. He writes a man named Heber Snell, who worked for the Church Education System as an Institute teacher, and he subsequently gets fired and I think reinstated because some of his controversial teachings, allegedly on the Old Testament. His name is Heber Snell.

He writes Heber Snell, and he said, "What does the scriptures say about the ban?" So, he recognizes Snell as an authority figure, and Snell has a Ph.D. from Chicago Divinity School in Old Testament studies I think, or something, back in the day when the CES used to send people back east for secular training.

GT: There was a great article, I'm trying to remember where that was,[32] called The Chicago Experiment.[33] Was he part of that?

Matt: He was.

---

[32] The article was by Casey Paul Griffiths and was published by BYU Studies. See https://byustudies.byu.edu/

[33] A brief summary can be found at https://mormonheretic.org/2011/07/16/the-chicago-experiment-a-fundamentalist-modernist-battle/

GT: That is really cool.

Matt: There was a few of them: T. Edgar Lyon, a guy named….

GT interrupts: Sperry.

Matt: Sidney B. Sperry, Russel Swenson, and Heber Snell. Yes, there was like five or six of them that go back, and he was definitely one of them. Anyway, I'm getting off topic here, but Snell writes a book that they wanted to use in the CES system. I can't remember the title of it, the *Ancient Israelite Heritage* or something. Anyway, Joseph Fielding Smith thought it was too secular. Some of the other apostles loved it, and thought it was great. Clearly it was informed by his training at Chicago Divinity School, and his study of Semitic languages.

Anyway, he was controversial for this CES system that was becoming increasingly orthodox after World War II. They wanted to try him for his membership at one point, and Sterling McMurrin and President McKay, I think, stepped in and said to Joseph Fielding [Smith], "We're not going to cut this good man off."

So, word gets out to Monroe Fleming that this guy is an authority figure in the scriptures, and he wanted to know from Heber Snell, what did the scriptures say about the priesthood ban? Snell, by the say, did not believe in the ban. It is very clear that he didn't think it was justified scripturally. He didn't think it was humane, a whole number of things. So, I think Monroe Fleming felt a kindred spirit in reaching out to Heber Snell.

He also sent a couple of letters to other people expressing his disappointment with not being able to hold the priesthood. In the meantime, publicly he is meeting with missionaries at the old Hotel Utah where he worked, and he is bearing his testimony. "This is God's church, and I know that the ban is inspired." So, he is having this challenge: saying one thing in public and saying something in private. Anyway, when the ban is lifted, he is one of the first black men to be ordained to the Melchizedek Priesthood.

GT: Oh, wow.

Matt: [He is] not the first. I think a guy named Joseph Freeman is on record.

GT: I think he lives here in Colorado, I believe.

Matt: Does he? Ok.

GT: in Denver, I believe, or he used to. I don't know if he still does.

Matt: I think you are right, yes. He would be a nice guy to interview.

GT: I would love to.

Matt: Yes.

GT: I was wondering if you knew him.

Matt: No, I don't. I wish I did. I don't.

GT: Ok.

Matt: I have his book though, *In the Lord's Due Time*.[34]

Anyway, Monroe Fleming was one of the ones that they ordained first. It is interesting. A lot of the general authorities who grew up and came of age in church

---

[34] Can be purchased at https://amzn.to/2IGMVXp

leadership with this ban, they recognized the hardships that the ban posed on people and families.

President Monson, the current church president was very close to Monroe Fleming, and he told Monroe Fleming's family, his daughters, this would have been in the early '80s, '83 in fact. Monroe Fleming, I think died in '83. Then apostle Monson told Fleming's family, and his secretary in the apostleship, the Quorum of Twelve, "If I am away on church business when this man passes, I am going to come back, drop everything, and I will be back to his funeral." Strangely enough, he was away on church business. He got the call and he came back, and he spoke at Monroe Fleming's funeral.

GT: Wow.

Matt: There are some personal relationships that the brethren will develop with these black Latter-day Saints. I just read this, that they feel compassion that the church is shutting them out. I'm just jumping the gun for a moment. A number of apostles will reach out to some of their personal relationships after the revelation is listed, to let them know first: "You are hearing it from me. We lifted this."

GT: Oh, wow.

Matt: Yes. There is a handful that do this. Gordon Hinckley is another one. They take a personal interest in some of the suffering that these black saints have had under this ban. Just one last thought along these lines: when the revelation is lifted, of course the biggest church leader to fight this for years was Hugh B. Brown.

It cost him his position in the First Presidency. He is dropped from the First Presidency for his very vocal proselytizing, crusading if you will. Anyway, he is dropped, and it crushes him. He is upset by this, and he is on the outs with some church leaders to be perfectly honest. But his heart was pure, and Brown dies in 1975. Three years later when the revelation occurs, of course he is not around, and N. Eldon Tanner, Gordon Hinckley, and a new apostle named James Faust, they call independently. They call Brown's family, including his grandson with whom I have spoken, and they say, "Your grandfather would have loved to have seen this day." This is hours after the revelation, the same day.

Of course, that is tacit acknowledgement of the bitter battles that Grandpa Brown, President Brown had fought to get this ban lifted. These three brethren, N. Eldon Tanner, James Faust, and Gordon Hinckley recognized it and wanted to acknowledge that to the family. I take that as a way to heal old wounds too. We come full circle. So, I thought that was kind of a moving moment when I read the transcripts of the calls.

GT: Wow.

Matt: Yes, because a relative gave me the transcripts.

GT: Is that going to be in your book?

Matt: Yes.

GT: Oh, wow. I will be one of the first to buy that book.

Matt: Yes, I have so much material that has never been seen before and it is such a moving story in many ways, with black people in the church, white people. Because they just have this policy. The church has boxed themselves in, and they don't feel like they can move it or change it. They agonize over it.

You see this when you read their journals. Spencer Kimball, I have gone through his journals and I have been very privileged from his family to see those journals and the Church Archivist. Really, it is moving to see his journals because when he is an apostle in the 1960s, part of his jurisdiction is over South America. So, he is visiting these branches and these wards, and he talks about this in his journal. He is a great diarist. These South American saints will come up to him after the meeting and say, "I pay my tithing. I am faithful. When can I hold the priesthood?"

It just crushes Elder Kimball, who recognizes that this branch needs priesthood leadership, and these are faithful people. But yet, this policy has shut them out. He agonizes over it, completely agonizes over it.

So, it is not surprising that when he is the church president, here is something provocative for you. When he is the church president, the first thing he wants to do is to lift the ban. He has all of these experiences that he has gathered. Keep in mind in the fall of '69, he has already agreed to lift the ban. He has already gone on record to his son in the letter that he writes to his son Edward in 1963, he said, "I think this ban might be a possible error."

GT: Really?

Matt: It is the word he uses.

GT: In '63.

Matt: In '63, a possible error. So, he has been wrestling with this ban for a while. Anyway, he has already agreed to lift it. He has already had all of those experiences in South America, but he has got some challenges. He has got the same challenges that President McKay had. He has got some doctrinal hardliners. He has got people in the South who have some very deep-rooted racial views.

GT: So, it is interesting to me that you say that was one of the first things that he was going to do was lift it, because if I remember correctly, it seems like at his first news conference, just like Harold B. Lee's news conference, one of the first questions was, are you going to lift the ban? He said, "I have no plans to do so."

Matt: Oh, I know what he said.

GT: So, you say that he really was going to do that right away?

Matt: Yes, yes.

GT: It was 1974 when he was named church president?

Matt: Was it December of '73, I think when he was ordained? I think December, late '73, yes.

GT: So, I mean that's another 4 years, so if that is the first thing he is going to do, why does it take four years?

Matt: Ah, that's a great question. So, President Kimball is a great student of church history, and he has lived through the David O. McKay years, which were very contentious, with all due respect. President McKay, his declining health over the years had created a power vacuum, really. There were some folks who argued the First Presidency counselors really should be making firm decisions for the church, and others thought it should revert back to the collective body of the quorum.

You see this happen in church history a lot.[35] You saw it happen in the '80s with Gordon B. Hinckley when Marion G.

---

[35] See our interview with John Hamer:
https://gospeltangents.com/2018/01/13/different-succession-claims-mormon-groups/

Romney and N. Eldon Tanner were incapacitated, along with President Kimball. Arguably, I don't know about today but maybe you see it happening with Thomas S. Monson. Does President Eyring or President Uchtdorf call the shots, or is it the senior leadership in the Twelve? The guy that is going to be the next church president. So, you do see these sorts of very difficult things pop up and I think Greg Prince says nicely,[36] and Gary Bergera has written some articles about how contentious some of these years were with factions vying for power.

But President Kimball has witnessed firsthand some of those challenges from the '50s and '60s from President McKay's leadership. There were schisms in the quorum to be honest. He was part of those schisms. But more importantly, he looks back at President Wilford Woodruff's administration, where he has a revelation, lifts the …{pauses}

GT: polygamy.

Matt: …polygamy, the First Manifesto,[37] issues the First Manifesto. You're a student of church history. You know what happens. Half the quorum falls away.

GT: My current interview is with Anne Wilde right now.[38] That is exactly what we are talking about.[39]

Matt: Oh, nice, nice. I like her. She's a gem.

---

[36] See our interview with Greg Prince at https://gospeltangents.com/2017/11/27/4-leadership-vacuums-happened/
[37] For more background, see our interview with BYU professor Dr. Richard Bennett: https://gospeltangents.com/2017/04/16/ouija-boards-spiritualism-manifesto-endowments-for-the-dead/
[38] See https://gospeltangents.com/2017/10/25/taylors-1886-polygamy-uncanonized-revelation/
[39] See https://gospeltangents.com/2017/10/29/woodruff-marry-1890-manifesto/

So anyway, President Woodruff doesn't get buy-in from the Twelve. This is "God spoke to me and we're going to issue this Manifesto, and we're going to end polygamy."

Of course, the brethren and the Twelve are split. You know the story, half of them get excommunicated, and they start to replace them with monogamists, like David O. McKay. So, when McKay comes in 1906, the guy who he is replacing is a polygamist. So, the litmus test is, you're a monogamist, right? {chuckles}

So anyway, Kimball knows the consequences of doing something unilaterally without quorum buy-in. He sees that in church history, and he experiences it himself in the McKay administration. So, President Kimball recognizes this is such a delicate task, and if he is going to make this, arguably, probably the most momentous—not arguably. In the 20th century, it is the most momentous decision in the history of the church, second maybe only to plural marriage, giving black people the priesthood.

So, he knows he has to have buy-in. How do you get buy-in from people who have very, very deep-seated racial views? I mean Elder McConkie's *Mormon Doctrine*,[40] he comes into the Quorum of the Twelve in 1972, but yet he had been this very larger than life personality, even before he is an apostle, writing this controversial book called *Mormon Doctrine* that is published in 1958.

So, he is worried about the doctrinal hardliners. He doesn't have Harold B. Lee or Joseph Fielding Smith to contend with, but he still has Mark E. Peterson and Bruce R. McConkie, and he has some other general authorities who

---

[40] Can be purchased at https://amzn.to/2lExVcT

are products of their generation. They have some hard views about people of color.

GT: Elder Benson?

Matt nods: Elder Benson. We will talk about him in a minute. Yes, it is true. Elder Benson and Delbert Stapley is another one that has some very hard racial views. But anyway, President Kimball, I think this is really the genius of his leadership. One of the first things he does is he recognizes you have to get buy-in from the Twelve. How do you do this?

He uses a variety of things, really. One of the things he does is he announces a temple in Brazil. Oh gee! I mean it is like 85% bi-racial. Ed Kimball, I love Ed. I love his work, and he wrote something in that book[41], like his father was just oblivious to the racial—or something like that. I interviewed Ed years ago. He is really a wonderful man. I said, "Oh Ed. Your father knew the racial makeup. He had been there as an apostle." He just kind of gave me that Ed Kimball twinkle. I have nothing but respect for that man, and his father.

But anyway, President Kimball announces the Brazil Temple. This is a bulwark to help the brethren to come along with this. He recognizes that you can't have temple in this heavily bi-racial nation, where the people who sacrificed and do so much to build the temple are shut off from it. I mean he understands this. This is just not good policy.

"We're going to make you sacrifice and work so hard." Those are the days when you built it yourself. You didn't

---

[41] Edward Kimball wrote a biography about his father called *Lengthen Your Stride*. See https://amzn.to/2LmAuC6

have Salt Lake writing you a check. So, these guys are donating. They are really sacrificing hard to build the temple, and they can't go. Helvicio Martins, the late general authority, this is his story. He does so much to build this temple, and he is shut off by it. Kimball is there, and he pulls Martins. He had heard from other people, James Faust who is a general authority in charge of Brazil at the time. He heard from Brother Faust that "We've got this wonderful negro man named Helvecio Martins. He really is one of the finest in the church. Kimball meets him at the dedication of the Brazil Temple, and he tells him: "Remain faithful. Good things will happen." I am paraphrasing, but there is something coming.

GT: What year is this approximately?

Matt: This is '75 maybe. Was it the cornerstone?

GT: '75, ok.

Matt: I think so. Don't quote me on that.

GT: Three years earlier, roughly.

Matt: So, President Kimball is saying something pretty early on to Martins. Maybe it is a year later. I don't recall, but it might have been the foundation or something. I don't think it was the final dedication. I'll have to look at that.[42]

But anyway, the Brazil Temple is a way to "let's try to help the brethren understand that we've got to do something here."

GT: So, this was very strategic.

---

[42] The Brazil Temple was announced March 1, 1975. Construction began a year later, and it was dedicated on October 30, 1978 by President Kimball.

Matt: Yes, very much so. One of the first things he does as president is to push for this Brazil Temple. It is not coincidental.

Bruce R. McConkie Wrote Official Declaration 2!

Matt: The other thing is, he announces this incredible vision for the church that we need to universalize the Mormon message, the gospel message. That means every kindred, nation, tongue, and people.[43] There is no footnote that says, "Except black nations, African nations." It means every; "every member a missionary."[44]

Keep in mind, the church had tried an experiment in the previous decade, the '60s to put missionaries in Nigeria. It fails miserably, because Nigerians are upset that they have to have white leadership from Utah, this American nation, to run our churches. Why can't we run our own?

They don't have the priesthood. So, it's an experiment. I think the brethren tried opening up a mission in Nigeria, just to see if it would work. It didn't work. A lot of issues that I am going to write about...

GT interrupt: This is what Greg Prince talks about.

Matt: Prince talks about it a little bit, yes.

GT: In 1962?

Matt: Yes, yes. A guy named Lamar Williams is the guy from Utah who is over there to shepherd this work. So, I

---

[43] This is a reference to the Book of Mormon. See Mosiah 15:28 at https://www.lds.org/scriptures/bofm/mosiah/15.28

[44] President David O. McKay seems to be the source encouraging "every member a missionary." See https://www.youtube.com/watch?v=3fjtmCCunBl or https://www.lds.org/manual/teachings-david-o-mckay/chapter-6?lang=eng

will write about that. There are some interesting details in Nigeria.

So, with President Kimball, he has got the Brazil Temple. He has got this great vision of universalizing the gospel message. He is going to send a *Mars Candy* executive named Merrill Bateman, who will later become a general authority and president of BYU. Bateman had spent some time in Africa. In the 1970s, he calls Merrill Bateman in, and he tells Bateman essentially, "I'm going to send you to Africa. Just let me know about the people there who are sympathetic towards the church." They had some branches there at the time. "Let me know about their strength." Bateman has no idea what is going on. He tells Bateman, "Don't tell anybody about this, nobody. This is just between you and me, not even my counselors."

GT: Wow.

Matt: So, Bateman comes back and gives a report. By this time his counselors were invited to the meeting. Clearly President Kimball had shared it with President Romney and Tanner. Bateman gives a [report]: "We have got a couple of guys there that went to BYU." There is a handful of Africans who went to BYU back in the '60s, over Ernest Wilkinson's protests {chuckles}, another whole story. He said, "They are faithful. They are smart. They are intelligent. They could run the church."

"Thank you, Brother Bateman."

So anyway, I haven't talked to Merrill Bateman. I can't imagine he didn't know what was going on, but who knows? Maybe he didn't. So, President Kimball is doing some reconnaissance work in Africa. If we lift this ban, they are going to know that these people can run the church. So, he gets this very heartening report from Merrill Bateman, who was a member of the *Mars Candy Corporation*. He had spent some time there working for *Mars* doing some business, and that is why he was asked to go.

Also, going on behind the scenes is President Kimball's meeting with a man named Jack Carlson. He is Ph.D. in economics from Harvard. He is a liberal Mormon democrat. He is one of the proud three in the '70s! {chuckles} He works in the Carter Administration. He calls Jack Carlson into his office, and just has this very candid discussion. This is in I think '76-77, somewhere in there. He calls in Jack Carlson and his wife, just the three of them: President Kimball and the Carlsons. He says, "Jack, why do the Carter people hate us so much?"[45]

He said, "President, don't you get it?

"No, tell me. That's why you are here."

He said, "They hate our views on ERA, our views towards women and ERA." This is in the midst of the ERA movement. Of course, Utah was the holdup, arguably one of the states that kills the amendment, to be honest. The church was against it, and that galvanized opposition. "The other thing is, they don't like our views towards black people."

President Kimball, without missing a beat, says, "We've got to change this policy, but I can't. I am worried. I am worried about how the saints in the South will take this

---

[45] Matt misspoke. Carlson did graduate from Harvard, but did not serve in the Carter Administration. Carlson served in the Nixon and Ford Administrations, and was a republican. He ran unsuccessfully against Orrin Hatch for senate in Utah in 1976. See his obituary at https://www.nytimes.com/1992/12/08/us/jack-carlson-59-budget-specialist-and-ex-us-aide.html

policy." It's the same thing McKay had to deal with, you remember? "I am worried about my brethren in the Twelve." That's what he said.

GT: What year is this again?

Matt: This is '75-76. He is just telling this. There is nothing prayerful about this. There was not, "I am going to have a revelation. I am going to have to pray to the Lord and see what he says." I mean he was just speaking very pragmatically. "We need to lift this ban. I've got this vision for the church, and I can't fulfill this vision as long as we can't get into African nations. But I have got a problem. I have got members of the Twelve who have don't support it, and I have got members in the South. Who knows what is going to happen?"

So, anyway, [there are] little bits and pieces going on here and there. Here is where the story really just increases my admiration for President Kimball. He will meet with the apostles one by one, and in group meetings. This is a great exercise in interpersonal leadership, organizational leadership as they say. So, President Kimball will meet both collectively and individually with each of the apostles, and he will ask them to produce written accounts of their views about the ban. Elder McConkie of course, writes an account too, as you can imagine. He has got some feelings about it.

GT: He just pulled chapter whatever out of *Mormon Doctrine*, right?

Matt jokes: Right. Go see chapter so-and-so. I've already covered that! Go read the book. Buy the book!

But anyway, it is kind of a funny story. Elder McConkie, "I can see that we have a problem with the Brazil Temple. I have got a solution. We should lift the ban!" {Matt chuckles}

GT: That's what McConkie said?

Matt chuckles: Yes.

GT: Really!

Matt: It's a really great story because of course President Kimball has understood this much earlier, but needed to get Elder McConkie's buy-in. So, Elder McConkie, "I've got the solution. We need to lift this ban to help our Brazilian brothers and sisters out."

I'll just pause for a moment. Joseph Fielding McConkie, his son who taught at BYU for years, died in, I think, 2013 of cancer. But anyway, he wrote a memoir, or biography of his father that Deseret Book published in 2003. On the chapter on the priesthood revelation, Joseph Fielding McConkie gives credit to the revelation, as I read it, to his father.

GT: Oh, really?

Matt: Yes. I chuckle with this because President Kimball knows what he is doing. He needs to get Elder McConkie's buy-in. When he gets Elder McConkie's buy-in that the ban needs to be lifted, I mean he feels that there is a tremendous weight off his shoulders.

This isn't to take away of course any of the spiritual aspects of the temple and the revelation, and the things that the apostles will recount afterwards about it being the most magnificent spiritual experience of their life. I think that's all very authentic and genuine, but it just speaks to President Kimball's remarkable leadership, that I order to do this, "I've got to really work with my associates and massage them and help them to understand that this is the right thing to do." To me that is just an incredible, remarkable exercise in leadership on President Kimball's part, because he doesn't want to create a schism in the Twelve like President Woodruff had under his leadership.

I am sure as the church president that President Kimball could have just done something unilaterally. But if there is no buy-in, what is the point? Right? If people don't feel that this is the right thing to do, that's really one of the most remarkable things is that he gets the buy-in from Elder McConkie. What is equally remarkable is, not only is there buy-in from Elder McConkie, the biggest doctrinal hardliner, but it is Elder McConkie who writes the Second Official Manifesto that will be added to the Doctrine & Covenants. That is his language.

GT: Oh, that is McConkie?

Matt: Yes.

GT: Oh really?

Matt: They asked three people, as I recall, to write letters when the revelation happened. Elder McConkie, Elder Thomas S. Monson, and Boyd K. Packer. Each of those men had submitted their drafts to the First Presidency, and they chose Elder McConkie's.

GT: Oh wow! That's really interesting.

Matt: Yes. Anyway, there is a lot of stuff going on, but that is the upshot. The last thing is the Genealogy Department just got deluged with requests from the mission field. "We have got this brother. He has got black blood. What do we do?"

There was a growing sense, at least among some general authorities, "We can't lecture President Kimball and tell him what to do," but the church work was so difficult with these kinds of things. I will just tell you one quick story.

There was a woman in Mexico, a sister missionary, and she had been out for I think, 15 months. It's an 18-month mission, so she is on her tail end. Anyway, she discovered that she had African ancestry, and she is almost done. So, her mission president writes, a guy name Tom Fyans, who was the General Authority Seventy over that mission. "Dear President Fyans, what do I do?

Fyans writes back to the mission president, "What kind of a missionary is she?"

"Oh, she is most faithful and she is an effective missionary and bears a strong testimony."

"How much time does she have left?"

"[She has been out] about 16 months."

Fyans writes back, "I think you should take about four or five months and study the issue." {Matt chuckles}

I mean this is going on a lot in the church, and it is going on in branches when you have got branch presidents who have got negroid blood, and they are great branch presidents, and they have the affection of their ward or their branch, and all of the sudden, "Oh! I have got African ancestry."

So, they see this a lot. It weighs on President Kimball, and it weighs on other authorities, so it creates a—the First Presidency secretary will say this after the revelation. He goes on record and he will say that "the priesthood revelation lifted a collective sense of guilt the brethren had felt over the years." I think I got that quote exactly right.

GT: Hmmm, ok.

Matt: "It lifted a collective sense of guilt the brethren felt over the years."

GT: Wow.

Matt: Yes. This was Francis Gibbons, who wrote lots of biographies about church presidents.[46] He was the church president during the revelation, or I'm sorry, President Kimball's secretary. That's what he said, "It lifted a collective sense of guilt the brethren had felt over the years."

GT: Wow, it must have been, because I have heard other stories about people. In fact, I'm trying to remember if that was one of your presentations last year or not. Somebody, and I want to say it was from either BYU or the Church History Library, or something, that said somebody in, I want to say Panama, that he went to the bishop and said, "I want to be ordained," or the branch president.

And he said, "You're black, you can't."

He went to his mom and she said, "You're not black," and so he told the branch president, "[My mom] said [I'm] not black."

The bishop said, "Oh, ok, we will ordain you."

Was that your presentation?

Matt: I am not sure.

GT: Or not your presentation, but it was in that same session?

---

[46] For a list of books by Gibbons on church presidents, see https://amzn.to/2Lye5So

Matt: Maybe, yes.

Matt: It's ad hoc, really. Without going into details, you get some instances of church leadership where a bishop confesses: "I just learned that I have black ancestry."

The presiding authority says, "Ok. Carry on brother."

"What?"

"Yeah, you heard me. The Lord needs you."

"Ok."

And then you get other instances where, "Oh, I'm so sorry to hear that, so you must stay your hand." That was a nice idiom that meant, we're going to have to release you from your calling as bishop. You can't exercise your priesthood publicly. You must stay your hand, but you can exercise it privately in your own home.

GT: Oh, wow.

Matt: Yes, then there are a couple of instances that I know of where they release the bishop. The ward is upset. They love this bishop, and after about a year and a half when there is nobody to really fill in the gap, they [say], "Ok, we have lifted it." This is like 1968. "You can be the bishop again. You don't have to stay your hand anymore."

So, I am not trying to make light of this important thing, but once again it speaks to the pragmatic effects of this policy. They need good priesthood holders in these units in South America. We haven't even talked about other places like Australian aborigines and Fijians on the Pacific Islands.

GT: From what I understand, they were not considered African and therefore not descendants of Cain, and therefore could be ordained, especially Fiji and Australia.

Matt: That is correct. This is 1950s when President McKay did a lot of research into this. In Fiji, when they started to open up the mission, we talked about after World War II expanding, well part of that expansion meant the Pacific islands. It took them a long time to develop missions in the Pacific Islands, even well into the 1970s, and even '80s.

But they get into Fiji I think in the '50s, and of course the question is, these are dark-skinned Fijians. Can they hold the priesthood? Are they from Africa, their ancestry? They don't know. The First Presidency, they are getting letters from, as you can imagine, they get letters from the mission field. What do we do? The missionaries are wondering, shall we baptize them? Should we confirm them to the priesthood?

They turn to the church scriptorian, Joseph Fielding Smith. Brother Smith, do they have African ancestry? He writes this lengthy letter back. This is, I think, 1954 to the First Presidency and he says, "I've done a lot of research. I have looked at the *Encyclopedia Britannica*. I have looked here. I have looked there. I can't tell you. I am at a loss."

So, what happens is, some local leaders will go to the Fijian Institute Museum, or something. It is some local museum in Fiji. They meet with some anthropologists, these LDS leaders in Fiji, and they ask these anthropologists, are Fijians descendants of Africans. They say unequivocally, "No." They share that evidence with President McKay. Once he sees the evidence, especially since President

Smith can't determine it, then he says, "Ok. Green light. Let's ordain these folks."

GT: Wow.

Matt: This is like 1958. What is interesting about this whole ban is, of course it is based on—I think this is important for your listening audience to know, it is based on bloodline, not skin color. So, it is possible to have a blue-eyed, blond-haired person with African ancestry, so blue-eyed, blond-haired, fair-skinned with African ancestry, and they can't hold the priesthood because of their lineage.

Then you can have this very dark-skinned Fijian who can hold the priesthood. It really creates—I'm going to create a word here today, but a racial no-man's land if you will. Because I am going to give this one story where this LDS man who fell into that category, he was white, fair-skinned Caucasian, and he had African ancestry supposedly, and he goes in to Joseph Fielding Smith, and he said, "I'm torn. I'm crushed. I want to serve a mission. What should I do? I want to marry a woman in the temple."

President Smith looks at him and he says, "I don't have anything for you. I don't know what to tell you."

This man was agonizing because he said, "I'm not a negro. Look at me. I am not a negro, and I don't feel comfortable marrying a negro, but yet I can't marry a Caucasian woman because I can't take her to the temple, and I want to take her to the temple."

President Smith just basically [said], "I don't know what to tell you."

Anyway, it is controversial.

GT: The thing that I want ask about that, because we talked a little bit about the one-drop, or one-quarter rule was if this person looked white, I wouldn't think a grandparent would have been black, so it would have been farther back than that.

Matt: Probably, yes.

GT: So, I mean if we are following the old slavery rule about one-quarter, it looks like it did go more to the one-drop rule.

Matt: Yes.

GT: As time when on with the priesthood ban.

Matt: Yes, I don't remember in this particular case. I don't know where his ancestry went, if it was further back. I just remember from the interview, "I can't hold the priesthood. I am agonizing over this. I want to hold the priesthood, and I can't."

GT: Would it make sense that it was farther back than grandparents though, for this ancestry?

Matt: Yes, often times the restrictions went further back than grandparents. So, what would that be? You're the math guy. 1/25th would be grandparents, 1/16th, 1/8th, the further we go back.

GT: Well let's see. 1/4th would be grandparents.

Matt: 1/4th, yes, one-quarter would be grandparents.

GT: 1/8th would be great-grandparents. 1/16th would be great-great-grandparents.

Matt: 1/16th would be great-great-grandparents. These racial laws were created in the 20th century. They would be fluctuating between 1/16th, 1/8th, and 1/4th.

GT: That is what the U.S. law did.

Matt: Yes, the church, though, what is interesting about this in the 20th century, the church did follow the 1/4th rule, the quarter rule I guess as they called it, they also called it the one-drop rule, that if you have one-drop. Now there is no fraction involved with one-drop, right? Now if you have got one-drop, you are disqualified.

GT: You can go back eight generations, and all of the sudden, oh, I'm now disqualified.

Matt: Yes. That's why, not to go off topic, but one of the reasons why Hugh Nibley had a problem with the ban is if you go back far enough, everybody has negroid blood, he wrote. So, that was the one-drop rule, is that you would be penalized for grandparents and that sort of thing.

This guy, I guess we can deduce that clearly it wouldn't have been a grandparent that was from African origin, but further back. So, it creates a hardship when you have got dark-skinned people who can hold the priesthood, and light-skinned people who look Caucasian, and they look white but yet they are banned from the priesthood and the temple.

GT: Wow, that's strange.

Matt: It is a tough one, yes.

Additional Resources:

To learn more about Black History, check out our previous interviews:

Newell Bringhurst – Author on early black Mormon History
130: Walker Lewis: Faithful Black Elder
https://gospeltangents.com/2018/02/26/walker-lewis-faithful-black-elder/

129: Warner McCary: Real Native Genius?
https://gospeltangents.com/2018/02/25/warner-mccary-real-native-genius/

128: How Lester Bush Debunked the Missouri Thesis
https://gospeltangents.com/2018/02/18/how-lester-bush-debunked-missouri-thesis/

127: Writing Saints, Slaves, and Blacks
https://wp.me/p8l6gx-oQ

Russell Stevenson – Biographer of Elijah Ables
126: The LDS Church in Africa
https://gospeltangents.com/2018/02/12/lds-church-in-africa/

125: Elijah Ables' Attempt for Temple Blessings
https://wp.me/p8l6gx-ox

124: Why Brigham Changed his mind on Black Ordination
https://wp.me/p8l6gx-ou

123: Trouble in Cincinnati: Ables' Time in Ohio (Stevenson)
https://gospeltangents.com/2018/02/04/trouble-cincinnati-ables-time-ohio/

122: Ables' Canadian Mission & Escape from the Mob (Stevenson)
https://gospeltangents.com/2018/02/01/ables-canadian-mission-escape-mob/

121: Early Life of Elijah Ables (Stevenson)
https://gospeltangents.com/2018/01/29/early-life-of-elijah-ables-blackhistorymonth/

Darron Smith on Race, Religion, & Sport

035: Overcoming "Nice" Racism (Smith)
https://gospeltangents.com/2017/05/16/nice-racism/

034: BYU Protests (Smith)
https://gospeltangents.com/2017/05/13/byu-protests/

033: How do Minorities fare at BYU? (Smith)
https://gospeltangents.com/2017/05/10/how-do-minorities-fare-at-byu/

032: True & False Rape Allegations at BYU (Smith)
https://gospeltangents.com/2017/05/07/true-false-rape-allegations-at-byu/

031: How BYU Could Improve the Honor Code for Black Students(Smith)
https://gospeltangents.com/2017/05/04/how-byu-could-improve-the-honor-code-for-black-students/

030: Black Graduation Rates at BYU (Smith)
https://gospeltangents.com/2017/05/02/comparing-byus-black-graduation-rates/

029: Disparities in Black/White Discipline (Smith)
https://gospeltangents.com/2017/04/28/disparities-in-blackwhite-discipline/

028: The Student-Athlete Business (Smith)
https://gospeltangents.com/2017/04/25/the-student-athlete-business/

027: Racial Portrayals of Christian Athletes (Dr. Smith)
https://gospeltangents.com/2017/04/22/racial-portrayals-of-christian-athletes/

Mark Staker on Black Pete

011: Black Pete's Mormon Mission in 1831 (Staker)
https://gospeltangents.com/2017/03/05/black-petes-mormon-mission-in-1831/

010: Black Pete: The First Black Mormon (Staker)
https://gospeltangents.com/2017/03/03/black-pete-former-slave-becomes-first-black-mormon/

Dr. Paul Reeve on Black Mormon History in Utah

009: <u>Dr. Paul Reeve's Role in Race Essay</u>
https://gospeltangents.com/2017/02/27/paul-reeve-wrote-the-race-essay/

008: <u>Dating the LDS Temple and Priesthood Ban</u> (Reeve)
https://gospeltangents.com/2017/02/26/dating-the-lds-priesthood-and-temple-ban/

007: <u>Becoming a Fanboy of Orson Pratt</u> (Reeve)
https://gospeltangents.com/2017/02/24/becoming-a-fanboy-of-orson-pratt/

006: <u>The Black Mormon Scandals</u> (Reeve)
https://gospeltangents.com/2017/02/22/the-black-mormon-scandals/

005: <u>How did Joseph Smith Deal with Muslims?</u> (& Chinese & Indians?)
https://gospeltangents.com/2017/02/19/how-did-joseph-smith-deal-with-muslims/

004: <u>How did Others Deal with Slavery?</u> (Reeve)
https://gospeltangents.com/2017/02/12/how-did-others-deal-with-slavery-blackhistorymonth/

003: <u>How Mormons Became a Racial Category</u> (Reeve)
https://gospeltangents.com/2017/02/09/how-mormons-became-a-racial-category/

Margaret Young on Jane Manning James

002: Margaret also discusses her experiences <u>combating racism in Part 2</u>
https://gospeltangents.com/2017/02/02/race-is-a-touchy-subject-blackhistorymonth/

001: <u>Biography of Jane Manning James</u> (Young)
https://gospeltangents.com/2017/01/29/is-there-no-blessing-for-me/

Epilogue

I hope you enjoyed of our conversation with Dr. Matt Harris. We're concluding our discussion of the priesthood and temple ban, but I'll bring back Matt later to discuss his upcoming books on President Benson. Since we're talking about priesthood, I wanted to keep the conversation going, but talk a bit about women blessing the sick. Dr. Jonathan Stapley has a new book that discusses priesthood from a theological angle. In our next conversation, we'll introduce the common idea of priesthood and motherhood. What does Dr. Stapley think about that?

Jonathan: Mormons have created a dichotomy oftentimes between priesthood and motherhood, which I talk about in the book, and which I think isn't particularly historical. It is historical in the sense that it's been around for a while, but doesn't make a tremendous amount of sense in our tradition.

Click here to subscribe (on iTunes), click here for a transcript. (You can also get one at Amazon.com), and over here you'll see some other videos that we've done on Youtube.) We hope you'll use this as a valuable resource to learn more about Mormon history!

We'd also love to have you visit our Amazon Store on our website to see other books on Mormon History. Be sure to check out our blog as well at https://GospelTangents.com to find information about future guests and projects we are working on. We would also like to partner with artists and musicians to produce a documentary on this and other topics. Please email us at GospelTangents@gmail.com if you're interested.

Thank you for your generous support!

9 781983 064289